MW01173269

KNOW YOUR WHY

Dr. Susan Nordin

DR SUSAN NORDIN

Know Your Why

© 2024 by Dr. Susan Nordin

All rights reserved.

This book is protected under the copyright laws of the United States of America. This book may not be copied or reprinted for commercial gain or profit. The use of short quotations or occasional page copying for personal, or group study is permitted and encouraged. Permission will be granted upon request.

Dr. Susan Nordin
PO BOX 752963
Houston TX 77275

Translations Quoted:
AMPC—Scripture quotations taken from the Amplified® Bible (AMPC), Copyright © 1954, 1958, 1962, 1964, 1965, 1987 by The Lockman Foundation Used by permission. www.lockman.org
ESV—Scripture quotations are from The ESV® Bible (The Holy Bible, English Standard Version®), © 2001 by Crossway, a publishing ministry of Good News Publishers. Used by permission. All rights reserved.
HCSB—Scripture quotations marked HCSB are taken from the Holman Christian Standard Bible®, Copyright © 1999, 2000, 2002, 2003, 2009 by Holman Bible Publishers. Used by permission. Holman Christian Standard Bible®, Holman CSB®, and HCSB® are federally registered trademarks of Holman Bible Publishers.
KJV—Scriptures marked KJV are taken from the KING JAMES VERSION (KJV): KING JAMES VERSION, public domain.
MSG—Scripture quotations marked MSG are taken from The Message, copyright © 1993, 2002, 2018 by Eugene H. Peterson. Used by permission of NavPress. All rights reserved. Represented by Tyndale House Publishers.
NIV—New International Version, Copyright © 1973, 1978, 1984, 2011 by International Bible Society, Zondervan Publishing House. Used by Permission
NLT—Scripture quotations marked (NLT) are taken from the Holy Bible, New Living Translation, copyright ©1996, 2004, 2015 by Tyndale House Foundation. Used by permission of Tyndale House Publishers, Carol Stream, Illinois 60188. All rights reserved.
NKJV—Scripture is taken from the New King James Version®. Copyright © 1982 by Thomas Nelson. Used by permission. All rights reserved.
TPT—Scripture quotations marked TPT are from The Passion Translation®. Copyright © 2017, 2018, 2020 by Passion & Fire Ministries, Inc. Used by permission. All rights reserved. ThePassionTranslation.com.

VOICE—Scripture taken from The Voice™. Copyright © 2012 by Ecclesia Bible Society. Used by permission. All rights reserved.

YLT—Scripture quotations marked (YLT) are taken from the 1898 YOUNG'S LITERAL TRANSLATION OF THE HOLY BIBLE by J.N. Young, (Author of the Young's Analytical Concordance), public domain.

TABLE OF CONTENTS

DEDICATION

I dedicate this book, first and foremost, to the One who created me on purpose for a purpose, my Lord and Savior, Jesus Christ.

I dedicate this book to my husband, Don Nordin. He is my best friend, my greatest support, my biggest comfort, and my strongest motivation. I have learned to value and welcome your unique perspective on anything I am walking through. You have held me steady in so many ways. Every love story is beautiful, but ours is my favorite.

I dedicate this book to my Revival Group. During our Sunday afternoon meetings in my home, they allowed me to guide them toward discovering their individual identities and purposes. That rich fellowship launched me into the rewarding ministry I have named "The Purpose Process." It has resulted in hundreds of people, ages 17 to 84, discovering their unique identities and life purposes. I wish to offer a special dedication to one group member, Derek Heron. He is the first person I have led in crafting a purpose statement.

The Revival Group's positive energy and success inspired the Kingdom Leaders Academy (KLA) birth. KLA leads people toward the discovery of their identities and purposes and their God-ordained spheres of influence in the world.

Finally, I dedicate this book to Nick Caveness, who helped me formulate my "here-there" path. That effort enabled me to acquire focus, set goals, and gain significant momentum toward reaching some specific benchmarks, among which was publishing this book.

My purpose statement is:
"I am reparenting a generation in identity and purpose for legacy's sake."

FOREWORD

Here is another exciting book from the fertile mind and heart of Susan Nordin! *Know Your Why* will build and bless you in every paragraph. One excerpt from page 22 leaps right off the page and shows us what is here for the taking:

> *"Your blessings are not ahead of you; they are behind you, but you will pull them toward you as you walk in His will. That means that everything that is for you will come looking to find you as you walk in your purpose."*

Susan is extraordinary! She carries a strong desire for the Lord and His Word, is an ardent student of Scripture, and is an exemplary exegete, interpreter, and teacher of it. She is Senior Leader of a megachurch, Community Transformation Church, in Houston, Texas. She and her husband, Don, are one of the finest and most successful ministry couples in America.

I am honored and pleased to be asked to write the foreword for this splendid book. Like her other books, it is easy to read, filled with exciting revelation of the Word, and extremely helpful for students, teachers, and ministers of the Bible, as well as leaders in every profession.

However, this book is even more. I have observed Susan at work over the years as pastor and teacher of hundreds of developing leaders in every walk of life as she enables them to deeply understand and concisely and meaningfully express what they sense their reason for existence to be. It is this actual experience in her extensive workshop that has birthed this book, a leader's treasure that he or she will consult over and over again.

Susan made use in this book of her knowledge of both Greek and Hebrew to clearly express her ideas. She is a careful wordsmith who handles the Scriptures accurately and reverently.

Her insight in chapter three that God works out our beginning and formative years from his knowledge of our end or fulfilled purpose is eye-opening, inspiring, and more than worth the price of the book. Her extensive use of many different translations of Scripture adds a richness to this book not found in many. Chapter four is a powerful study showing that each of us is "a word from The Word". It contains insights into identity, purpose, calling, anointing, and assignment.

I could go on and on, but you will find much more as you read and reread these pages. You will thank me for recommending this book for your personal and professional development, whether you are in ministry, business, or one of the professions.

Ronald E. Cottle, Ph.D., Ed.D. D.D.

Founder, Christian Life School of Theology

Founder and President of Embassy College

INTRODUCTION

One of my favorite quotes is, *"You are here on purpose for a purpose."* I fully believe that you arrived on the planet with your purpose embedded, and it is molded through your life experiences.

Most people know they have a purpose. However, when asked what it is, they need help formulating a sentence that describes it clearly and concisely.

For years, I have been fascinated with books and studies about purpose. I have read countless books on the subject, many effectively convincing one that one has a purpose. Yet, I have found none that offer a formula for expressing it in words.

I have made it my mission to craft a formula that enables people to express meaningfully and concisely what they sense in their hearts regarding their reason for existence.

This book springs from my personal study of God's Word. It is derived from volumes of notes I have compiled in diligent pursuit of understanding how to gain a clear perspective on one's identity and purpose. It contains the formula the Heavenly Father has revealed to me to accomplish that.

I view people on this journey of discovery as puzzle solvers. As I share the truths I have discovered, I have observed that they can pull the pieces together, revealing a coherent picture of their personal "Why?"

I pray that as you embark on this magnificent journey of learning how to put the pieces of your puzzle together, you will see clearly how God intends for your life and efforts to bring value to others.

CHAPTER 1
A WHISPERED WORD

Do you have a word from God that he has spoken directly to you?

> **Psalm 119:11 (NKJV)** says, "Your word have I hidden in my heart, that I might not sin against you."

Most people think this verse refers to memorizing the Bible, but that's not what it means at all. It does not refer to the whole Bible.

The Hebrew word translated "word" in this verse is "*imrah.*" It is derived from another Hebrew word, "*amar.*" The Greek version of this Hebrew word "*imrah*" is "*rhema.*"

Another Hebrew word for "word" is "*dabar,*" which is translated into Greek as "*logos.*"

Debar is a general word that means principles for all. An example would be the Ten Commandments. *Debar* is a universal word, a written word, and a proclaimed word. It refers to direct, clear, and forceful speech.

Amar is a more personal word, a particular word, a whispered word, a secret word. It describes everyday conversation that comes from the Lord's heart to an individual's heart.

Amar is a spoken, private word. It is a particular word to a specific individual. It is whispered words. It is orders given. It is His intention for us.

"Your Word have I 'hid' in my heart..."

A SAFETY DEPOSIT BOX

The Hebrew word for "hid" is "*tsaphan*" and in Greek it is "*thesaurus.*"

What is a thesaurus? It is a treasury of words wherein all the words in a language are enumerated: the antonyms, synonyms, the adverbs, the adjectives, verbs, the nouns, and everything in that particular language.

This Hebrew word, "*tsaphan,*" could be considered akin to a safety deposit box. What do you put in a safety deposit box? You put in it precious valuables or important documents—personal possessions that matter greatly to us. *Tsaphan* means to store up and treasure.

"Your word have I hidden in my 'heart." Our heart is where the whispered, secret word from God is stored. Our heart is where the battle for that whispered word happens.

"Your word have I hidden in my heart, that I might not 'sin' against you."

"Sin" in Hebrew is the word "*chatta.*" In Greek, it is the word "*hamartia.*"

One of the amazing meanings of "*hamartia*" is "to miss the mark." It's like shooting for a bullseye on a target and missing.

YOU HAVE A DIVINE DESIGN

So, with all these meanings combined, you could paraphrase **Psalm 119:11** to say: "The divine design that you have spoken to me I have treasured it in my innermost being so that I might not miss the mark or bullseye of your purpose and calling on my life, that you have declared to me."

This verse conveys a powerful revelation and deep meaning. It speaks to our purpose and design, which God has whispered into us to communicate his intention for our lives.

Now, I want to show you something powerful about Mary, the mother of Jesus.

When Gabriel told Mary she was "highly favored," he used the Greek word "*charitoo.*"

This word is only used in one other place in Scripture. Check this out! This word is found in **Ephesians 1:6 (ESV):** *"To the praise of his glorious grace, with which he has blessed us in the Beloved."*

The word "blessed" is the translation of the word "*charitoo*" in the original. This is the same word that was used to describe what happened to Mary as she was chosen to carry in her womb the Word, our Lord Jesus Christ.

I never thought of myself as someone as special as Mary, but I am! Like Mary, I am chosen to carry his seed, my own *rhema* word, and to birth it! And so are you!

This is speaking of mine and your purpose. God has "*charitooed*" us in Christ!

WE CARRY THE RHEMA WORD

We are chosen to carry our own *rhema* word, that whispered, specific word to us. We should hide these words in our hearts and carry them until we give birth to them.

Did you notice in this story of Mary that she "pondered" this? Where? "In her heart!"

In **Luke 1:38 (KJV)**, when Mary said: *"Be it unto me according to thy word,"* guess what she was referring to? The *"rhema"* word.

Looking back at **Luke 1:37 (KJV)**, Mary states, *"For with God nothing shall be impossible."* The word "nothing" in this verse is also the word *"rhema."* This verse means that no *"rhema"* word will be without *"dunamis"* power.

When the angel speaks all of this to Mary, the Scripture states that she is *"troubled in her heart"* **(see Luke 1:29)**. She is surprised to hear such extravagant words, especially about her.

She was surprised by the wonder of the Creator God speaking such extravagant words to her. That *"rhema"* word left her awestruck.

You and I are chosen to carry our own extravagant word. That whispered, specific word was spoken to us, and we have hidden it away in our hearts.

Mary first responded with surprise to what the angel said about her. As soon as she realized this was an assignment God gave her, she agreed without objection. She accepted, complied, and submitted to God's plan for her life. Pay close attention to these words of faith... *"Be it unto me according to thy (rhema) word"* (Luke 1:38 KJV).

Mary:

- She had Faith.
- She received the Word.
- She birthed the Word.
- She endured ridicule.
- She raised Jesus.
- She never received a second Word.

One Word lasted thirty-three and one-half years – and for the rest of her life!

I believe we are born with our purpose—that *"rhema"* word already embedded in our being. It is like an internal GPS that constantly speaks and pulls us in the direction God intended for our lives.

This "*rhema*" word is where we find our fulfillment in life. I challenge you today to uncover that whispered word spoken to you in eternity before you ever arrived on this planet.

Psalm 119:11 (My paraphrase):

> "My divine design that you have spoken to me, I have treasured it in my innermost being so that I might not miss the mark or bullseye of your purpose and calling on my life that you have declared to me."

Like Mary, let's also say, *"Be it unto me, according to your word."*

CHAPTER 2

AWAKENED TO PURPOSE

What time is it in our world?

If you are spending time watching mainstream media, you may be experiencing anxiety, worry, and thinking that the world is falling apart.

You are learning about the issues that face our world today. Here are a few to consider:

- Worries about the supply chain and food security (gas and food shortages).
- Major forthcoming issues in the financial markets regarding inflation, the national debt, the worldwide debt, and the stock market bubble.
- Illegal immigration.
- Political upheaval around the world.
- The threat of wars.
- The pandemic.
- Drug addiction. A recent study shows that 41 million Americans are struggling with addiction.
- Racism.

- Child abuse.
- Trafficking, otherwise known as modern-day slavery. An estimated 5.5 million people worldwide are trafficked, with 25% of those being minors.[1] In Texas alone, it is estimated that there are 313,000 victims of trafficking, with 25% of that number representing minors.[2]

With that in mind, think of this: God is the one who matched you with this day and time! He created you for this moment.

The Pew Research Center states that Christians remain the world's largest religious group, making up nearly one-third or 31% of the earth's 7.3 billion people. What if one-third of the 7 billion people on Earth decided to find their purpose and live it? What kind of impact would we have?[3]

---

[1]*Sex Trafficking in the U.S.: A Closer Look at U.S. Citizen ...*, Polaris, polarisproject.org/wp-content/uploads/2019/09/us-citizen-sex-trafficking.pdf.

[2] *More Than 300,000 Estimated Victims of Human Trafficking in Texas,* The University of Texas at Austin - Steve Hicks School of Social Work, 11 Oct. 2020, socialwork.utexas.edu/more-than-300000-estimated-victims-of-human-trafficking-in-texas/.

[3] Hackett, Conrad. *Christians Remain World's Largest Religious Group, but They Are Declining in Europe,* Pew Research Center, 5 Apr. 2017, www.pewresearch.org/short-reads/2017/04/05/christians-remain-worlds-largest-religious-group-but-they-are-declining-in-europe/#:~:text=Christians%20remained%20the%20largest%20religious%20group%20in%20the,to%20a%20new%20Pew%20Research%20Center%20demographic%20analysis.

YEAST THAT PERMEATES THE DOUGH

The Bible compares us to yeast and the world to dough. And yeast always permeates the dough. That is what can happen when we walk out our purpose.

I want to awaken you to your purpose today and challenge you to become the yeast that permeates the dough.

Here is what I've come to understand about purpose - You arrived here pre-approved. Let me show you this through the following scripture.

Ephesians 1:18 (NKJV)

> [18]I pray that the eyes of your understanding be
> enlightened; that you may know what is the
> hope of his calling, and what are the riches of
> the glory of His inheritance in the saints.

In verse 15, Paul starts a prayer, asking that the eyes of our understanding be enlightened so that we may know or understand what's already inside of us. He is praying that we would act based on understanding our position in Christ.

In other words, Paul prayed that you would act based on who you are in Christ, which is your purpose.

Then he states, *"That we may know the hope of his calling."* Note that it is His calling, not ours. It's His calling in us. God has placed a calling inside you. We are to be confident, expectant, and to have a sense of certainty. We are to possess a confident hope of His calling.

YOU HAVE A CALLING

Now, let's look at the word "calling." It is the Greek word *kaleo*. It means to call aloud, to utter with a loud voice, to invite, to name, to bear a name or title (among men). It is taken from the base word, *keleuo*, which means to command and order at one's command or bidding.

The phrase "in the saints" is *en humon.* Its meaning indicates that God has placed a calling inside us—a command, an order, a bidding. It's that urging, prodding, and expectancy inside that God has invested in us.

It is our greatest possibilities, our finest potentialities, and God puts it inside us.

God told Jeremiah, *"Before I formed you in the womb, I knew you"* **(see Jeremiah 1:5)**.

"Before" in Hebrew is *terem*. And it means: not yet; before that; to interrupt or suspend.

This means that before conception, I was suspended in eternity. I existed before the moment of conception.

God says to Jeremiah, "I knew you." The word "knew" is the word *yada* in Greek.

To "know" something is to properly ascertain it by seeing it. It means to make exact, certain, or precise; to find out something; to make certain of something; to find out or learn with certainty.

One resource I use that explains Hebrew words said this about *yada*[4]: to *yada* means more than knowing about something or someone. It's more than mental knowledge. The Hebrew word "know" (*yada*) can mean "enter into covenant together."

---

[4] Hegg, Tim. "Hebrew Word Yada." *Torah Resource*, 8 May 2024, torahresource.com/article/hebrew-word-yada/.

But why would the word "know" (*yada*) be used to denote a covenant relationship between two people?

This is because a covenant between two people or a king and his people in the ancient Near East formed a relationship that could not be broken. Any breach of that covenant would result in severe consequences (the curses of the covenant).

So, we could interpret what God said to Jeremiah as: "I covenanted with God, while suspended in eternity, until the exact moment I was needed on earth for a precise purpose."

Acts 17:26-29 (TPT)

26-29From one man, Adam, he made every man and woman and every race of humanity, and he spread us over all the earth. He sets the boundaries of people and nations, determining their appointed times in history. He has done this so that every person would long for God, feel their way to him, and find him —for he is the God who is easy to discover! It is through him that we live and function and have our identity; just as your own poets have said 'Our lineage comes from him. Since our lineage can

be traced back to God, how could we even think
that the divine image could be compared to
something made of gold, silver, or stone,
sculpted by man's artwork and clever
imagination?

Lineage is the Greek word "*genos*," meaning kindred, family, or taken from his genes.

Have you ever ordered one of those ancestry kits and traced your genealogy?

Many people trace their ancestry as far back as human records allow. But our lineage far surpasses that. According to these verses in Acts, our roots run all the way back to the kingdom of heaven.

My own personal ancestry shows that my ancestors came from England, but I know that God as my Father is my true source, and my lineage traces back to the kingdom of heaven. I am a daughter of the living God!

Having ancestors from England has never gotten me anything from God. My roots run way past England—all the way back into eternity. I am a daughter of the living God.

Psalm 139:16 (HCSB)

[16]Your eyes saw me when I was formless; all my days were written in Your book and planned before a single one of them began.

Your mom and dad made you, but God created you.

2 Timothy 1:9 (HCSB)

[9]He has saved us and called us with a holy calling, not according to our works, but according to His purpose and grace, which was given to us in Christ Jesus before time began.

What was given to us? Purpose and grace were given to us. When? Before time began.

2 Timothy 1:9 (VOICE)

[9]God has already saved us and called us to this holy calling—not because of any good works we may have done, but because of His own intention and because eons and eons ago (before time itself existed), He gave us this

grace in Jesus the Anointed, the Liberating
King.

GOD HAS A PLAN FOR YOU

What is written about you in His book? Purpose and grace are.
Purpose is what is written in His book concerning you.

Grace is the empowerment to actualize your purpose, to
bring it into the reality of the earthly realm.

We, on earth, must decide if we will obey what Heaven
intends. We must AGREE with His plan.

Ephesians 1:4 (TPT)

4In love He chose us, in Him before the
foundation of the world. That we should be holy
and without blame before Him in love.

This is not an exhortation to us. Instead, this is a declaration
about us.

Psalm 139:16 shows us God is the omniscient Master
Architect. He formed me in my mother's womb placing within
me free will - the ability to make my own choices - and then
played not just every day of my life out, but according to verses

1-5, he knew my every thought and my every word before I ever came into being.

That's why we agree with verse 6, *"Such knowledge is too wonderful for me; It is high, I cannot attain it."* In other words, that should blow our minds.

There are massive buildings in downtown Houston near where I live. I am pretty positive that no one just drove over to Home Depot and purchased a pickup truckload of materials during the construction of these buildings.

Instead, there were teams of people who planned the placement of every bolt and screw long before the first one was ever bought.

Before the building was started, they planned for torrential rains, hurricane-force winds, and every other contingency.

It was built on paper before it was ever built downtown!

AND SO WERE YOU!

This is what **Psalm 139:16** communicates to us. We were made, and our lives were lived out on paper, in the pages of the book that God used to write out each day of our lives before we were ever formed in our mother's womb.

Romans 8:29-30 (HCSB)

[29]For those He foreknew He also predestined to be conformed to the image of His Son, so that He would be the firstborn among many brothers. [30]And those He predestined, He also called; and those He called, He also justified; and those He justified, He also glorified.

Those verses list a five-step process of identifying and bringing God's intentions onto the earth.

1) **"Foreknew"** is the Greek word *proginosko*, and it means "to foresee, foreordain, to know before."
2) **"Predestined"** is the Greek word *proorizo*, which means "to determine before."

Predestined: Pre means "before," derived from the root word of *horizo*, derived from our English word "horizon." So, "predestined" means to mark out our horizon, to appoint, decree, or ordain.

Destiny is the actualized purpose of something. He planned the end from the beginning.

Isaiah 46:10 (NIV) states: *"I made known the end from the beginning, from ancient times, what is still to come. I say, 'my purpose will stand, and I will do all that I please.'"*

3) **"Called"** is the Greek word *kaleo*, which means to give us a command or order, to surname.

4) **"Justified"** is the Greek word *dikaios*, which means "righteous" or "keeping the commands of God." This word is also used for someone whose way of thinking, feeling, and acting is wholly conformed to the will of God and who, therefore, needs no rectification (to be made right) in the heart or life.

5) **"Glorified"** is the Greek word *doxazo*, which means: "full of glory."

Psalm 8:5-6 (TPT) states:

5-6Why would you bother with puny, mortal man or care about human beings? Yet what honor you have given to men, created only a little lower than Elohim, crowned with glory and magnificence. You have delegated to them rulership over all you have made, with everything under their authority, placing earth itself under the feet of your image-bearers.

Psalm 40:6-8 (HCSB)

⁶You do not delight in sacrifice and offering;
You open my ears to listen.
You do not ask for a whole burnt offering or a
sin offering.
⁷Then I said, "See, I have come;
it is written about me in the volume of the
scroll.
I delight to do Your will, my God;
Your instruction lives within me."

In that verse, Jesus was prophesying over Himself. Jesus has a book in heaven. What He was saying is that the law is written in My heart. That is a powerful statement. This means whatever is written in your book is also written in your heart.

Look in your heart if you want to discover what's in your book. Search out your:

- Desires
- Aspirations
- Longings

- Passions

WHAT PAGE ARE YOU ON?

Those hold the clues as to what's written in your book in heaven. Satan is terrified that we will discover what is in our book because he knows we will do massive damage to his territory when we step into all that heaven has ordained. So, he keeps us frustrated with his accusations!

What page are you on in your book of destinies?

CHAPTER 3
FINISHED BEFORE STARTED

Isaiah 46:9-10 (AMPC)

9[Earnestly] remember the former things, [which I did] of old; for I am God, and there is no one else; I am God, and there is none like Me, 10declaring the end and the result from the beginning, and from ancient times the things that are not yet done, saying, My counsel shall stand, and I will do all My pleasure and purpose."

God finished you before he started you. God's plan for your life is already finished. What you were born to do is already completed.

God was telling Isaiah to remember this, to keep it in his mind, and not to forget it.

He said the same thing three times:

1) I am God, and there is none like me. Don't forget that.

2) I am God, and I always set the end before the beginning. Don't forget that.

3) I tell from ancient times the things not yet done; my purpose will stand.

God is telling us that He always sets the end first. He decides who you will be and what gifts and abilities you will carry. He decides what ethnicity you will be and what epoch you will live in. After all that, He backs up and begins on your birthday.

That means God is finished before he starts. God completes a thing before He commences it. God is letting us know that when you see Him start something, it is evidence that it's already finished.

God would not allow you to be conceived unless there was something already finished that you were born to start!

A PREDETERMINED END

This means we begin on our birthday with the end already predetermined. This proves we were not mistakes; we entered the world with an already finished destiny. All we have to do is live according to His plan—this, of course, is entirely up to us.

God never begins with a beginning but with an end. He puts the period in the final sentence of our story, and then the story gets played out on the earth! So, your success is already finished. God says, "I set the end before I begin, and I make known at the beginning what the end will be." That's why, as a child, you dreamed all the time. That was your destiny screaming at you. Those dreams were real.

Don't ever judge your destiny by the location of your birth. Your parents had no idea who was growing up in their house.

The consequences of your birth are secondary to the purpose God has designed for you. Whether your parents were in wedlock, out of wedlock, behind the lock, or under the lock, that was of lesser importance to God than His reasons for creating you. It was time for you to get here! God chose the precise moment you would be born. You are chosen!

Abortion activists boast that they are "pro-choice." Anti-abortion activists label their position "pro-life." I like to think of it now as pre-choice! This means that when we mistreat, abuse, or reject another human being, we are rejecting God's own inheritance.

THE END FROM THE BEGINNING

Ephesians 1:11a (AMPC)

11In Him we also were made [God's] heritage (portion) and we obtained an inheritance.

Ephesians 1:4a (AMPC)

4Just as [in His love] He chose us in Christ [actually selected us for Himself as His own] before the foundation of the world.

Your future is destiny unreleased. Your future is God's past. He's already been there, and that is why you can have peace. The end is trapped in the beginning.

If you open an apple, you find seeds, and in those seeds are potential apple trees. There are apples in those seeds. The future of that apple is inside that apple. The future of the apple seed is inside the seed. God places the future of everything within itself.

Our attitude is that our future is ahead of us, but that's not true. Our future is not ahead of us; it's trapped within us.

You already possess your future. When? Now! Apples possess their seeds now, and seeds possess the apple trees now. And it is so with everything God has created. The future of a thing is within that thing.

When you approach life for this year, you must remember, "This year is already in me." So, this means you should be careful to invest your time with the right people rather than waste your time with the wrong people. Some of the things you've been putting up with, you can't put up with any longer. Forget the things that need to be forgotten. Doing so is critical for you to do what you're supposed to do this year. There are people and places from which you must disconnect in order to move toward (or into) what you are purposed to do.

God is committed to the future He placed in you. Your future is more important than your past.

Isaiah said it! "I am God, and there is none like me!" Why? He is the only individual who can set the end before He begins, finish things before He even starts them, and complete them before He commences. God never begins anything at the beginning. He ends it first, then He backs up, and He starts!

That means God completes your life first. Then He backs up and starts your life. This communicates that when He begins your life, it proves it's already finished. So, your future is, in actuality, God's past! He's already finished your future. He's just backing up to start your beginning, with the future already finished.

That's why God doesn't panic about anything! You don't panic when you're finished! You only worry when you are unsure about the outcome.

But if you've already completed the outcome before you start, there's no need to worry. God is not worried. That's why you already have a book with the end and the beginning in it...your Bible!

A PLAN IS ALREADY IN PLACE

Ephesians 1:11 (NIV)

[11]In him we were also chosen, having been predestined according to the plan of him who works out everything in conformity with the purpose of his will.

Your future is easy for God.

Predestined means the destination is set before beginning. Think of a vacation you took recently. Your destiny was set before you even started.

And notice in this scripture verse that it is "according to the plan," not "a plan," but "the plan." God says I have SET THE PLAN! He preset your destination, then He backed up and started your life.

This tells us that when you were born, your future was already finished, and God said, "I have a plan to get you there." Your purpose is your destination, but the plan is the route. God has a way to get you to your destination in your future.

God will always tell you your destiny (your purpose). He will tell you the destination, but He doesn't tell you the route.

Why?

When he begins you, the present doesn't look anything like the future you. You don't have the wisdom, maturity, dignity, or experience for that future. So, He must devise a route to prepare you for it. Your route is revealed in your stories and life experiences. The plan is to prepare you for that future.

Proverbs 16:9 (NIV) *"In their hearts humans plan their course, but the Lord establishes their steps."*

This verse shows that He doesn't tell you more than the next step.

Remember Joseph's route? God gave him this amazing dream about His purpose for Joseph's life. The very next thing that happened was his own family tore off his clothes (his coat of many colors) and threw him into a pit. Joseph didn't plan for this, but God said, "I'll use it to work on your maturity." Then he gets put in prison, and God has it all set up that a fellow prisoner will be used to introduce Joseph to his purpose.

You may feel like your life has been full of traps, pits, and prisons. But just like he did for Joseph, God will use all that to develop, mature, and train you for your purpose.

When God gave Joseph the dream, had he told him, "You will be on a throne, ruling, serving, and feeding your family that will one day come and bow down to you, but the route that will get you there will be full of traps, pits, and prisons," Joseph might have said, "No thanks, keep your throne and your money, I'm going to stay right here and be a shepherd over these smelly sheep because I don't want to take that route to get to my destiny."

As stated earlier, **Ephesians 1:11 (NIV)** says, *"In him we were also chosen, having been predestined according to the plan of him who works out everything in conformity with the purpose of his will."*

How many things? Everything!

Those words "works out" mean that he makes everything to conform. According to Webster's Dictionary, "conform" means "To comply with rules, standards & laws. To agree or be in harmony with."

Have you done some dumb things in your life? Have you made some bad choices? Have you taken some wrong roads in some of your decisions?

God is saying that you can bring your faults, mistakes, mess-ups, and wrong turns in life to Him, and He will work them all into a testimony and turn you into a world changer. God will turn your mistakes into miracles to bring you back into His purpose for your life.

It doesn't matter where you've been, what you've done, or who you've done it with. He wants to align everything with His purpose for your life. He will work it all in! He makes it all fit!

When you drive by a commercial construction site, at first you will only see mud, dirt, overgrown shrubs, and trees that need to be removed. You'll see heavy-duty equipment and cranes moving and lifting things out of the way so construction can begin.

Everything looks a mess. The construction site is dirty, ugly, and chaotic.

But right in the middle of that construction sight, in front of all the piles of dirt and mud, is a beautiful sign depicting the finished building.

The picture shows a nicely painted building, with cars in the parking lot and people walking along the sidewalk. There are trees, flowers, and shrubs.

This is a perfect example of exactly what God does with us. God finishes the building first and then puts it on your vacant property.

And people walk past you while you are five years old and ten years old, and even twenty and thirty years old, and they look at that sign and doubtfully ask, "That's you?"

They might only see mud, dirt, rocks, and overgrown grass. They don't see anything significant happening in your life at that moment. But God points to the sign and says, "That's you."

Why? Because He is finished.

You will notice that the construction workers on that site are laboring diligently. They are sweating, mowing, trimming, and moving dirt. All over that property, people are working hard. But in the builder's mind, that building is already finished. In other words, the master architect finished everything, then backed up and said, "Let's start." And that is precisely what God does with your life.

Now, on such sites, there is a construction office and some men walking around with the architect's plans rolled up under their arms. Those plans are supposed to be consistent with the picture on that sign.

WHAT IS YOUR PLAN?

Here's a question for you to ponder. Is the life you are building consistent with God's picture for your life?

Proverbs 19:21 (AMPC) *"Many plans are in a man's mind, but it is the Lord's purpose for him that will stand."*

You are working hard to make your life look how you want it to. But are you cutting corners that contradict God's plans for you? Are you working with the wrong plans?

Then, the city inspector shows up. Guess who plays that role on God's construction team? It is the Holy Spirit. He comes every day to check on the progress. And He asks questions like, "Are you happy?" Your answer will likely be, "No, I'm not happy." And He says, "I know, and it's because you are using the wrong plans. These plans don't match the picture on that sign. You are building the wrong building here. This is not the intention of the Creator."

The city inspector (Holy Spirit) frustrates you, doesn't He? He intentionally scrutinizes. But His goal is to make God's plans prevail over your plans.

He keeps asking if you're happy, and when you answer "No," He reminds you that it's because you are doing something you weren't born to do.

God doesn't throw away the plans you concocted. He uses them as a testimony and an opportunity to work a miracle in your life. It's an opportunity to show His power and to put you back into alignment with His purpose.

If you've messed up the plans, just bring your mistakes to your Heavenly Father and ask Him to conform you back to your purpose. He'll turn your mistakes into miracles and testimonies. God makes all things work together for your good because you are called according to His purpose.

Looking at the top of the construction site sign, you will notice the words "Coming soon."

You need to realize that for yourself. You may not look like the picture on the sign yet, but it's coming soon. Now you understand what "purpose" is!

There are a lot of messy areas in your life, just like that construction site. A lot of dirt must be moved, and overgrowth needs to be mowed and removed. A lot of dust is still flying around, but don't let that confuse you! Just check your picture and remind yourself that you're coming soon!

If you are off track in your life, just let Father God take you to the picture and show you that your destiny is already finished.

It is said of Jesus, *"For the joy that was set before Him, He endured the cross, all the shame, and all the hardship."* (**Hebrews 12:2**) Why? Because he had already seen his picture.

Once you've seen the picture, you can tolerate the noise of the bulldozers and all the dust.

You may even think you were born at the wrong time and to the wrong people. But remember, Ephesians 1:4 says He chose you in Him before the foundation of the world, which means purpose forced your conception.

Don't allow shame to rob you of your fame.

Ephesians 1:3 (AMPC)

³May blessing (praise, laudation, and eulogy) be to the God and Father of our Lord Jesus Christ (the Messiah) Who has blessed us in Christ with

every spiritual (given by the Holy Spirit) blessing in the heavenly realm!

Ephesians 2:10 (AMPC)

For we are God's [own] handiwork (His workmanship), recreated in Christ Jesus, [born anew] that we may do those good works which God predestined (planned beforehand) for us [taking paths which He prepared ahead of time], that we should walk in them [living the good life which He prearranged and made ready for us.

God ordained some things for this year, even before the earth existed, and they belonged to this year. God has been waiting for this year to arrive and for you to get yourself positioned so that you can access all He has ready for you.

God has already known everything you would need and prepared it for you. And all those blessings "in the heavenly realm" come at the exact moment they are required.

When you step into your assignment for this year, everything you need to walk into that assignment will become readily available. It was already reserved for you!

Say this: "Lord, everything is reserved for this year. Release it now and cause it to move toward me now."

Your blessings are not ahead of you; they are behind you, but you pull them toward you as you walk in His will. That means everything that is for you will come looking to find you as you walk in your purpose.

CHAPTER 4
A WORD FROM THE WORD

Acts 17:28 (KJV) *"For in Him we live and move and have our being...For we are also His offspring."*

Jeremiah 1:4-5 (AMPC)

⁴Then the word of the Lord came to me [Jeremiah], saying,
⁵Before I formed you in the womb I knew [and] approved of you [as My chosen instrument], and before you were born, I separated and set you apart, consecrating you; [and] I appointed you as a prophet to the nations.

Ephesians 1:11-12 (AMPC)

¹¹In Him we also were made [God's] heritage (portion) and we obtained an inheritance; for we had been foreordained (chosen and appointed beforehand) in accordance with His purpose, Who works out everything in agreement with the counsel and design of His

[own] will,

[12]So that we who first hoped in Christ [who first put our confidence in Him have been destined and appointed to] live for the praise of His glory!

Psalm 139:15 (AMPC)

[15]My frame was not hidden from You when I was being formed in secret [and] intricately and curiously wrought [as if embroidered with various colors] in the depths of the earth [a region of darkness and mystery].

Psalm 139:16 (HCSB)

[16]Your eyes saw me when I was formless; all my days were written in Your book and planned before a single one of them began.

Acts 17:26 (TPT)

[26]From one man, Adam, he made every man and woman and every race of humanity, and he spread us over all the earth. He sets the

boundaries of people and nations, determining their appointed times in history.

The Amplified Bible (Classic) says: *"determined [their] allotted periods of time and the fixed boundaries of their habitation (their settlements, lands, and abodes)."*

Psalm 139:14 (AMPC)

¹⁴I will confess and praise You for You are fearful and wonderful and for the awful wonder of my birth! Wonderful are Your works, and that my inner self knows right well.

Psalm 139:13 (AMPC)

¹³For You did form my inward parts; You did knit me together in my mother's womb.

Psalm 71:6 (AMPC)

⁶Upon You have I leaned and relied from birth; You are He Who took me from my mother's

womb and You have been my benefactor from that day. My praise is continually of You.

1 John 3:1 (AMPC)

¹See what [an incredible] quality of love the Father has given (shown, bestowed on) us, that we should [be permitted to] be named and called and counted the children of God! And so we are! The reason that the world does not know (recognize, acknowledge) us is that it does not know (recognize, acknowledge) Him.

Ephesians 3:14-15 (TPT)

¹⁴⁻¹⁵So, I kneel humbly in awe before the Father of our Lord Jesus, the Messiah, the perfect Father of every father and child in heaven and on the earth."

The Passion Translation footnotes states: Ephesians 3:15 Translated from the Aramaic. It could also be translated "the perfect Father of every people group." The Greek word for "father" and the word for "family" are quite similar, which indicates that every family finds its source in the Father.

Romans 8:29-30 (NKJV)

[29]For whom He foreknew, He also predestined to be conformed to the image of His Son, that He might be the firstborn among many brethren. [30]Moreover whom He predestined, these He also called; whom He called, these He also justified; and whom He justified, these He also glorified.

Romans 8:29-30 (VOICE)

[29-30]From the distant past, His eternal love reached into the future. You see, He knew those who would be His one day, and He chose them beforehand to be conformed to the image of His Son so that Jesus would be the firstborn of a new family of believers, all brothers and sisters. As for those He chose beforehand, He called them to a different destiny so that they would

experience what it means to be made right with God and share in His glory.

Ephesians 1:9-11 (TPT)

9-11And through the revelation of the Anointed One, he unveiled his secret desires to us—the hidden mystery of his long-range plan, which he was delighted to implement from the very beginning of time. And because of God's unfailing purpose, this detailed plan will reign supreme through every period of time until the fulfillment of all the ages finally reaches its fulfillment —when God makes all things new in all of heaven and earth through Jesus Christ. Through our union with Christ we too have been claimed by God as his own inheritance. Before we were even born, he gave us our destiny; that we would fulfill the plan of God who always accomplishes every purpose and plan in his heart.

A WORD FROM THE WORD

Ephesians 1:4 (NKJV)

⁴Just as He chose us in Him before the foundation of the world, that we should be holy and without blame before Him in love.

The Greek word for "chose" in this verse is *eklegomai*.

When you look at the breakdown of this word, it communicates a powerful truth. *Ek* means out from a source or origin. *Lego* is the verb form of the noun *logos*, and *mai* means: "I use" or "I am used."

Let's look at the word *lego*. Again, it's the verb form of the noun *logos*. John 1:1 (NKJV) says, *"In the beginning was the word (logos), and the Word (logos) was with God, and the Word (logos) was God."*

Logos is the written Word of God, the whole concept, and the person of Jesus Christ.

This means we are a verb from the whole concept or personhood of Jesus. We are a concept from the full concept.

A word communicates. This means I have something to say. I am a word from God. A verb is an action word.

When you combine all the roots of this word, *eklegomai*, you have, "I am used as an action out of the Word. I am used to be a word from the Word."

This means I was put here for my life to speak. I am a word about God.

The Greek definition from Strong's Concordance for *eklegomai* is to pick out, choose, to pick or choose out for one's self; choosing one out of many, i.e., Jesus choosing His disciples; choosing one for an office, of God choosing whom He judged fit to receive His favors and separated from the rest of mankind to be peculiarly His own and to be attended continually by His gracious oversight, i.e., the Israelites, of God the Father choosing Christians, as those whom He set apart from the irreligious multitude as dear unto Himself, and whom He has rendered, through faith in Christ, citizens in the Messianic kingdom.

You are the verb born from the *logos*! God chose you and wrote a book of destinies about you so that you could live out on earth.

Each of us is designed in unique ways. We all have the following:

IDENTITY

You are a characteristic of Christ in the earth. You "re-present" Him. Perhaps the best way to say it is you "re-presence" Christ in the world through manifesting your heavenly identity.

There's a word that describes you best at the core of who you are. It's your atmosphere word. It defines the atmosphere that you thrive in. And it's the atmosphere that you carry into other environments and situations. It's also where you fight your biggest battles. It's the place where the enemy attacks and tries to disrupt you the most.

Your identity is your "who."

PURPOSE

Your purpose is your "why." Can you put your purpose into a sentence?

Knowing your purpose means understanding that you arrived on this earth pre-approved. Your purpose is your inner GPS system, your inner Siri. You can never get fired from your purpose.

CALLING

A lot of people get "calling" confused with "purpose" and with what their title is in life. Many people confuse "calling" with "purpose," and they believe their title reveals their purpose. That is not what your calling is at all. If you were to go on Google and find a picture or image representing your leadership style, what would that picture be? Your leadership style is your calling. Your calling is your long-term impact. It's how you make your life matter. Where do you see fruit from your life? Your calling never changes.

> *"The gifts and callings of God are unchangeable."*
> *(see Romans 11:29)*

ANOINTING

Your anointing is "God on you." It's what happens when you show up. Your character and presence bring something to the situation and achieve things. You are a mobile tabernacle.

ASSIGNMENT

Your assignment can change. Your assignment adds experience to your life. You receive training and equipping in your assignments. Assignments are equivalent to seasons.

It causes problems when you confuse your calling with your assignment.

People say they were called to a certain job or church. But if that job ends, it leaves them confused and unsettled when it was probably just their assignment.

The church I serve at is not my calling; it's my assignment. My calling is to disciple others. I love to teach and see the fruit and impact of that teaching on others.

When I showed up at my church in Houston more than 20 years ago, I showed up to my assignment, and I came with identity, purpose, calling, and anointing. The latter will never change about me, but my assignment can and will.

UNDERSTANDING YOUR SPHERE OF INFLUENCE

This will help you understand your sphere of Influence (adapted from *Basic Training for Prophetic Activation* by Dan McCollam)[5].

Answer each question below with a check mark beside all that apply (there can be more than one answer) from the following list:

The seven mind molders of society are:

- Business
- Government
- Media
- Arts and Entertainment
- Education
- Family
- Religion (church, ministry)

---

[5] McCollam, Dan. *Basic Training for Prophetic Activation.* iWAR and Sounds of the Nation, 2012.

Now answer each of the following questions by placing a check mark beside one of the preceding seven molders to which it applies:

- ☐ Question 1: In what area have I seen the most significant amount of influence, favor, and authority?
- ☐ Question 2: In what areas do the task, results, and promotion come most readily to me?
- ☐ Question 3: Where have I seen the most success with the least amount of effort?
- ☐ Question 4: In what area am I motivated to work hard and persevere?
- ☐ Question 5: In what area do people most respond to my gift or input?

Take notice of the two molders with the most check marks. This shows you where your sphere of influence is located. This is where you have the greatest favor and an open door before you to impact culture with the kingdom.

Hebrews 10:11-13 (NIV)

[11]Day after day every priest stands and performs his religious duties; again and again he offers the same sacrifices, which can never take away

sins. [12]But when this priest had offered for all time one sacrifice for sins, he sat down at the right hand of God, [13]and since that time he waits for his enemies to be made his footstool.

The word "wait" in this verse is the Greek word *ekdechomai*, which means to wait for, to look for. This indicates that God is waiting us out. He is waiting for us to awaken to who we really are and what we carry. He is waiting for us to step into our assignments in our spheres of influence and to impact the earth with heaven's agenda thereby.

I recently attended a training that a company in Houston, Texas, does for their employees. Its purpose was to provide those employees with tools to uncover the thoughts that animate their reactions in various situations. During the training, the instructors cast light upon multiple personality types and styles of leadership. In the end, they used the acrostic GOWYA, which stands for GO ON WHO YOU ARE, to remind the participants to be true to themselves.

That is my challenge for you as you discover your identity, purpose, anointing, calling, and sphere of influence. Go on being who you are, and you will be a world changer.

CHAPTER 5
DESTINED FOR MORE

In **1 Chronicles 4**, there is a genealogy list. It is the genealogy of Judah. In verse nine, the genealogy pauses and mentions a guy named Jabez.

> [9]Now Jabez was more honorable than his brothers, and his mother called him Jabez, saying, "Because I bore him in pain." [10]And Jabez called on the God of Israel saying, "Oh, that You would bless me indeed, and enlarge my territory, that Your hand would be with me, and that You would keep me from evil, that I may not cause pain!" So God granted him what he requested (**1 Chronicles 4:9-10 NKJV**).

Notice that his mother named him. Normally, in that culture, the fathers named their children, not the mothers.

A NAME IS NOT JUST A NAME

Parents didn't just hand out names carelessly. Naming a child carried tremendous importance. The name usually carried prophetic weight based upon what the parents sensed God saying about the child. When they gave it, they did so with a great sense of destiny for the child.

Their name was an actual sound substituting for a phrase, pointing to the parent's belief that the child would become.

SOME EXAMPLES:

> *Daniel:* God is my judge.
> *Ezekiel*: God strengthens.
> *Isaiah*: God is salvation.
> *Samuel*: God has heard.
> *Benjamin*: Son of my right hand.
> *Immanuel*: God is with us.
> *Abraham*: Father of many.

The name carried the parents' hope for their child. When Jabez's mother named him, she didn't do it casually. It was something formed in her, and she gave it to him with the intention that this name would become the magnetic north that drew the child with intention.

At Jabez's birth, something happened that gave the mother great pain and sorrow. Sorrow entered her life, and she couldn't handle it. And in her grief, she assigned her pain and sorrow to her newborn child.

We are very good at this. When we have pain, we tend to pass it on!

This lady gave her child her pain. She named him "pain and sorrow," as if the situation had been his fault. And even worse, that name became his identity and destiny. It became his magnetic north. The focus of his life would be pain and sorrow. If Jabez lived up to his initial billing, he would bring pain and sorrow to himself and those unfortunate enough to come into contact with him.

This negative assignment was imprinted upon him. She implanted within her child the notion that he was responsible for the pain and sorrow she was experiencing leading up to his birth.

She said he was responsible for all the pain and sorrow of the family. "I should have never birthed you," she implied. She spoke to him, "You are an accident. You brought me sorrow. You'll always bring me sorrow, so I name you 'pain and sorrow!'"

This means that he was broken from birth with a name that was a lie. He was not responsible, but he didn't know that.

Did you know that children cannot revise such words? When you say something, it is truth to them. I can scrutinize what you say to me as an adult, but a child cannot correctly scrutinize what is said to them.

So, Jabez builds his life on this lie. But again, it was a lie. He was not the cause of the pain and sorrow his mother was experiencing, and he was not responsible for the pain and sorrow of his life or that of his family.

The tragedy is that no one told him any differently. So, he ventured into life with that inherited name. It is possible that if the father had been there, this wouldn't have happened to him.

It happened once before in the story of Rachel and Jacob. She named her second son Bennonai in her death, which means "son of my sorrow." But Jacob stepped in and said, "No way! We are not going to call him by that name. He is 'Benjamin,' which means, 'son of my right hand.'"

However, in Jabez's case, no one was there to stop his imprisonment with this name, and it became his identity. His own self-image crippled him.

So dark energy surrounded this boy, and because of his culture, he believed that God had placed this destiny upon him.

Just like Jabez, the words spoken over us impart a curse, along with the words we say to ourselves.

James lets us know that our words govern our entire life.

James 3:4-5 (AMPC)

4Likewise, look at the ships: though they are so great and are driven by rough winds, they are steered by a very small rudder wherever the impulse of the helmsman determines. 5Even so the tongue is a little member, and it can boast of great things. See how much wood or how great a forest a tiny spark can set ablaze!"

This same verse in the Message translation reads:

3-6A bit in the mouth of a horse controls the whole horse. A small rudder on a huge ship in the hands of a skilled captain sets a course in the face of the strongest winds. A word out of your mouth may seem of no account, but it can accomplish nearly anything—or destroy it! It

only takes a spark, remember, to set off a forest
fire. A careless or wrongly placed word out of
your mouth can do that. By our speech, we can
ruin the world, turn harmony to chaos, throw
mud on a reputation, send the whole world up
in smoke and go up in smoke with it, smoke
right from the pit of hell.

Make a note of these powerful analogies. Words are like a bit
in a horse's mouth, a rudder on the back of a ship, or a spark to
a forest fire.

TIED TO WHAT GOD SAYS

In times past, sailing ships had large wheels on deck that
guided the rudder. The steersman tied himself to the wheel with
ropes so that if the rudder was driven in an undesired direction
by contrary waves or current, he could exert sufficient force to
redirect it. He would have the final say.

We must be tied to what God says about us, not what people
say. Neither can we be tied to what we say about ourselves. By
the Spirit, we must replace our thinking with what God says.

So, this very sick lady passed her darkness onto her child,
Jabez. And it's possible that a very broken parent or some other

adult passed their darkness upon you when you were a child or young person. It is possible that they passed on their pain, failures, disappointments, and brokenness to you.

Jabez's mom couldn't handle her pain, so she passed it on and took the attitude that she would let somebody else deal with it.

But the Word declares that he was more honorable than his brothers, and he leaves his imprint upon history.

How did this happen? One day, he heard the truth. This was undoubtedly a revelation of the true God, and that revelation of truth exposed the lies.

Genesis 18:18 (NLT)

[18]For Abraham will certainly become a great and mighty nation, and all the nations of the earth will be blessed through him?

Genesis 12:2-3 (NIV)

[2]"I will make you into a great nation, and I will bless you; I will make your name great, and you will be a blessing. [3]I will bless those who bless you, and whoever curses you, I will curse; and

all peoples on earth will be blessed through you."

Isaiah 43:1-4 (Message)

[1-4]But now, God's Message, the God who made you in the first place, Jacob, the One who got you started, Israel: "Don't be afraid, I've redeemed you. I've called your name. You're mine. When you're in over your head, I'll be there with you. When you're in rough waters, you will not go down. It won't be a dead end when you're between a rock and a hard place— Because I am God, your personal God, The Holy of Israel, your Savior. I paid a huge price for you: all of Egypt, with rich Cush and Seba thrown in! That's how much you mean to me! That's how much I love you! I'd sell off the whole world to get you back, trade the creation just for you.

Jabez woke up to realize he had another name—the one God created and gave him before birth, not the one his mother gave him.

"I have called you by name," and believe me, God doesn't call anyone by the name of a curse or darkness. He has His own name for us. He never puts you down or calls you a curse word. He never speaks one demeaning word over any individual.

Somehow, Jabez found out that God had named him.

NO FUTURE TENSE

There is no future tense in the Old Testament Hebrew language. It only speaks in present tense. The translators changed it over the years, and it has impacted the way we read the Bible today. The whole of the Old Testament was written in present tense. It contains no statements in future tense. Sometimes the Hebrew writers would communicate in past tense, but only as it related to how prior events affected current ones.

The translators of our English versions of the Bible usually render the text about Jabez similar to the following:

1 Chronicles 4:10 (NKJV)

[10]And Jabez called on the God of Israel saying, "Oh, that You WOULD bless me indeed, and enlarge my territory, that Your hand WOULD be

with me, and that You WOULD keep me from evil, that I may not cause pain!" So, God granted him what he requested.

That type of rendering is incorrect and disagrees with the original Hebrew.

The Young's Literal Translation reads it correctly:

> [10]And Jabez calls to the God of Israel, saying, "If blessing you do bless me, then you have made great my border, and your hand has been with me, and you have kept [me] from evil — not to grieve me;" and God brings in that which he asked.

In simple language, Jabez was saying, "Seeing that You bless me, my border is great now!" It was a present reality. Jabez realized his border had been large the whole time. That God's hand had been with him the entire time. That God had kept him from harm this whole time.

The present tense changes everything!

We put the blessing in the future, but in the Hebrew language, it is present! It is now! Jabez said, "Lord, I've been blessed all along."

Guess what? That's not just true about Jabez; it's true for me and you, too.

Ephesians 1:3-6 (YLT)

> [3]Blessed [is] the God and Father of our Lord Jesus Christ, who did bless us in every spiritual blessing in the heavenly places in Christ, [4]according as He did choose us in him before the foundation of the world, for our being holy and unblemished before Him, in love, [5]having foreordained us to the adoption of sons through Jesus Christ to Himself, according to the good pleasure of His will, [6]to the praise of the glory of His grace, in which He did make us accepted in the beloved.

Jabez was in Abraham. He was blessed from the womb. God made a covenant with Abraham and said his seed is blessed, and through his seed, all the families of the earth shall be blessed.

Jabez was blessed in the womb because of God's covenant with Abraham.

God told Jeremiah something similar. In **Jeremiah 1:5**, He said, *"Before I formed you in the womb, I knew you."*

Knew is *yada* in Hebrew, meaning to make a covenant with (See Chapter 2).

That means before your mom and dad went out that fateful night for dinner and a movie, and nine months later, you appeared on the scene, you were blessed before the womb, blessed in the womb, and blessed from the womb.

LIVING UNDER A LIE

Jabez had been blessed from the womb, but it had been hidden under a pile of trash and lies and wicked words spoken to him. All these lies were word curses spoken over him. And somehow, one day, the light got through the trash pile, and faith awakened him to see what and who he really was. He was blessed in Abraham. And so, he prayed. He saw what he had, and he laid hold of it.

Jabez realized all the data he had been working with was based upon a lie. When he realized that the covenant included him, he realized that he was in Abraham when it was made, and there was nothing more to do than to accept his patriarchal blessing.

Jabez's prayer was intentional, one where he connected with the divine desire.

He says to himself, "If I am blessed (meaning he was awakened to the realization of that), this means You are now keeping me; You are now enlarging me; You are now blessing me."

Proverbs 10:22 (NKJV) tells us, *"The blessing of the Lord makes one rich and adds no sorrow with it."*

But you say that was Jabez, what about me?

Psalm 8:3-6 (TPT)

3-6Look at the splendor of your skies, your creative genius glowing in the heavens. When I gaze at your moon and your stars, mounted like jewels in their settings, I know you are the fascinating artist who fashioned it all! But I have to ask this question: Why would you bother with puny, mortal man or care about

human beings? Yet what honor you have given
to men, created only a little lower than Elohim,
crowned with glory and magnificence. You have
delegated to them rulership over all you have
made, with everything under their authority,
placing earth itself under the feet of your
image-bearers.

Look at verse five again. It reads, "You have made them a little lower than Elohim and crowned them with glory and honor."

Each one of the sons and daughters of God was:

- Crowned: *atár*; to encircle (for attack or protection); to surround and to crown.
- With glory: The Hebrew word is *kabód*, meaning weight, strength, power, ability, and "referring to God" (dignity, splendor)

In the Greek, the word for glory is *doxa*. It means opinion, judgment, and view. It's someone's estimate or opinion.

How did those words get in the definition of glory?

Because whenever you see something in its glory, you get the original opinion, judgment, or estimate of its worth. You are dealing with the true estimate of something or the true view of something.

Glory is anything manifested in its true essence, as God had it in mind when He made it.

"Glory" is God's opinion about something. It is his view on something. It is his estimate of a thing. It carries the value of heaven. It carries the appraisal of heaven.

Your Bible says that when we saw Jesus, we beheld the glory. This means Jesus is the true estimate and appraisal of a man or a woman. Jesus shows us what God thought about a man in the earthly realm.

I'm encircled with the opinion of God.

HONOR

- Honor is *jadar* in Hebrew and means weight, splendor, and majesty.

The Greek word for honor is *time* (pronounced tee-may). Look at its amazing meaning: Perceived value, worth, price;

what has value in the eyes of the beholder; the value, weight, and honor willingly assigned to something. A valuing, a price, to estimate, a valuing by which the price is fixed.

1 Corinthians 6:20 says this about you: *"You were bought with a price, so glorify God in your body."*

"Price" is the same word as honor—*time.* You were bought with perceived value and worth. Your value was in the eyes of the beholder.

So don't let shame rob you of your fame.

Galatians 3:28-29 (The Message)

28-29In Christ's family there can be no division into Jew and non-Jew, slave and free, male and female. Among us you are all equal. That is, we are all in a common relationship with Jesus Christ. Also, since you are Christ's family, then you are Abraham's famous "descendant," heirs according to the covenant promises.

They still called him Jabez. He kept the name Jabez but lived in contradiction of his name. Everything he did, said, and lived was contradictory. You can become a contradiction to the negative words that previously shaped you. Earthbound gravity pulls you down, but God's gravity pulls you up and seats you in heavenly places in Christ Jesus.

You were and are destined for more.

CHAPTER 6

IDENTITY EXCHANGE

Exodus 3:13 (NIV)

¹³Moses said to God, "Suppose I go to the Israelites and say to them, 'The God of your fathers has sent me to you,' and they ask me, 'What is his name?' Then what shall I tell them?"

God said to Moses, "'I AM who I AM.' This is what you are to say to the Israelites: 'I AM' has sent Me to you.'"

God also told Moses, "Say to the Israelites, 'The Lord, the God of your fathers—the God of Abraham, the God of Isaac, and the God of Jacob—has sent Me to you.' "This is My name forever, the name you shall call Me from generation to generation."

God told Moses, "My name is 'I AM.' This is My name forever. This name is a memorial to every generation."

Exodus 20:7 (NKJV)

You shall not take the name of the Lord your God in vain, for the Lord will not hold him guiltless who takes His name in vain.

I always thought that using God's name in vain meant using it as a swear word. While I still believe that is true, I want to offer another perspective on how we misuse God's "I AM" name.

Consider the following ways we use God's name in vain:

I am fearful.

I am useless.

I am worried.

I am lonely.

I am unworthy.

I am confused.

I am insecure.

I am a failure.

These are identity statements and ways that we use God's "I AM" name in vain. When the name of God is spoken, something in the universe is perpetuated forever.

Identity is a complicated thing, isn't it?

WE ARE GIVEN NAMES AND LABELS

We begin life with a name, both a given and a family name. Those names, for good and for bad, give us a heritage. We are given our family's past hurts and failures.

We are given predispositions to addictions or predispositions to skills and certain career trajectories. We are given wounds from abuse, we are given tendencies, mannerisms, and personalities, and we are given a family legacy, whether positive or negative.

Some studies have shown that our makeup consists of 80% identity and 20% nurturing. These studies go on to say that our identity comes from our father's presence in our lives and the nurturing from the presence of our mother.

As we grow, more definitions of our identities are given. Yes, we have our given names, but we have other names too:

We are labeled:

> Smart
> Hyper
> Needy
> Stupid

Athletic

Fat

Ugly

Annoying

Incompetent

Lazy

Talented

Thin

Selfish

Nerdy

Dumb

Attractive

Welcomed

Lovable

We carry the names we have been given on our backs like heavy boulders, step-by-step, as we grow from childhood into adolescence, through young adulthood, and into adulthood.

We unknowingly expend great effort trying to rename ourselves. We do incredible amounts of work attempting to overcome the names we've been given. Regardless of whether the labeling was intended to insult or compliment, we find ourselves engaged in activities such as studying harder, working later, drinking longer, being sexually promiscuous, or building walls in an effort to protect ourselves from being known.

With every hour spent studying, every salary bump, every sexual partner, every pound lost, every drug consumed, and every rehab attended, we're attempting to redefine ourselves.

We are attempting to wrestle control away from the darkness we've experienced and to redefine ourselves at the core.

The attempts we make to silence the naming voices, the haunting voices, and to heal our emotional wounds end up destroying us.

The names we give ourselves are as destructive as the ones given to us by others.

It doesn't have to be this way.

The world attempts to label us, then seeks to discard us and works relentlessly to degrade us. It repeatedly wounds us and rehearses our failures and faults aloud. But amid all that turmoil, we can be adopted into the family of a Father who declares his deep pride in us before heaven and earth!

We are not the names we've been given. We are not the past we've lived. Your past may explain you, but it doesn't have to define you. We are not even the future yet to arrive. We are sons and daughters of God, and in us, God is well pleased.

John tells us that while Jesus informed his disciples that He was going away, He made His great promise to send the Holy Spirit.

> [15]"If you love me, keep my commands. [16]And I will ask the Father, and he will give you another advocate to help you and be with you forever— [17]the Spirit of truth" **(John 14:15-17a NIV).**

"Advocate" is the English form of the Greek word *parakletos* (Strong's #G3875)[6] and It means an intercessor, advocate, or comforter.

But when you look at the word more closely, *Para* means to come alongside and speaks of the closest possible proximity of nearness.

Kaleo means to identify by name, to surname.

In **1 Thessalonians 5:11,** it is translated as "joint-genesis."

---

[6] "G3875 - Paraklētos - Strong's Greek Lexicon (NIV)." Blue Letter Bible, www.blueletterbible.org/lexicon/g3875/niv/mgnt/0-1/.

The use of the word *parakletos* reveals to me that my genesis is from God. And since he is our Heavenly Father, we need to know what he has named us.

1 John 3:1 (AMPC)

> ¹See what [an incredible] quality of love the Father has given (shown, bestowed on) us, that we should [be permitted to] be named and called and counted the children of God! And so we are! The reason that the world does not know (recognize, acknowledge) us is that it does not know (recognize, acknowledge) Him.

Ephesians 3:14-15 (TPT)

> ¹⁴⁻¹⁵So I kneel humbly in awe before the Father of our Lord Jesus, the Messiah, the perfect Father of every father and child in heaven and on the earth.

The footnotes in The Passion Translation for this verse states:

> *Ephesians 3:15 – Translated from the Aramaic. It could also be translated "the perfect Father of every people group." The Greek words for "father" and "family" are quite similar,*

indicating that every family finds its source in the Father.

Romans 8:29-30 (TPT)

$^{29-30}$For he knew all about us before we were
born and he destined us from the beginning to
share the likeness of his Son. This means the
Son is the oldest among a vast family of
brothers and sisters who will become just like
him. Having determined our destiny ahead of
time, he called us to himself and transferred his
perfect righteousness to everyone he called.
And those who possess his perfect
righteousness he co-glorified with his Son!

Did you see that? This verse plainly states that He "called us."
When that realization dawns on us, we discover that we aren't
what everyone else in life has called or named us.

NAMED BEFORE HE WAS BORN

Let me introduce you to a man named Cyrus.

Nearly 150 years before Cyrus's birth, the prophet Isaiah
foretold his birth, his name, and the tasks that the Creator God
had predetermined for him to accomplish.

Cyrus is mentioned more than thirty times in the Bible. History has labeled him "Cyrus the Great." He reigned over Persia between 539 and 530 BC. This pagan king is important in Jewish history because it was under his rule that Jews were first allowed to return to Israel after seventy years of captivity.

Later, Jeremiah read this 150-year-old prophecy to Cyrus.

(see) Isaiah 44:28

The LORD says of Cyrus, "He is my shepherd,
and he shall fulfill all my purpose."

God called him His shepherd. It is said that when Cyrus heard all that had been prophesied about him, he was seized by a holy desire to fulfill his destiny.

Do I have the same desire to fulfill what was written about me some hundreds of years before I was alive? Do you?

THINGS ARE WRITTEN OF YOU

> [7]"Then said I, Lo, I come: (in the volume of the book it is written of me), to do thy will O God."
> **(Hebrews 10:7 KJV, quoting Psalm 40:7)**

Paul took a verse that pertained to Christ alone and made it his own.

Did you know that "in the volume of the book, things are written of YOU?

Let me show you some examples of what is penned there.

It is written of me in the volume of the book that I AM:

A child of God - **Romans 8:16; 1 John 3:1**

Saved - **Ephesians 2:8; 2 Timothy 1:9**

Complete – **Colossians 2:10**

Chosen- **1 Thessalonians 1:4**

Forgiven - **Ephesians 1:7; 1 John 2:12**

A new creation - **2 Corinthians 5:17**

Redeemed - **Psalms 107:2; Ephesians 1:7**

Light – **Matthew 5:4**

Justified – **Romans 5:1**

Free – **Romans 6:22**

More than a conqueror – **Romans 8:37**

God's address (temple) – **1 Corinthians 3:16**

One with Christ – **1 Corinthians 6:17**

Called – **1 Corinthians 7:17**

Created for good works – **Ephesians 2:10**

Safe in Christ – **Colossians 3:3**

Victorious – **1 Corinthians 15:57**

Not condemned – **Romans 8:1**

Guarded by God's peace – **Philippians 4:7**

No longer a slave – **Galatians 4:7**

Accepted – **Romans 15:7**

An ambassador for Christ – **2 Corinthians 5:20**

Healed – **Psalm 30:2**

Surrounded by God's Mercy – **Psalm 32:10**

Flawless – **Song of Solomon 4:7**

Not alone – **Isaiah 41:10**

Strong – **2 Corinthians 12:10**

Blessed – **Psalm 84:4**

Special to God – **1 Peter 2:9**

Joyful – **Romans 15:13**

Alive – **Ephesians 2:4-5**

Precious to God – **Isaiah 43:4**

A Citizen of Heaven – **Philippians 3:20**

Wonderfully made – **Psalm 139:14**

Hopeful – **Jeremiah 29:11**

God's – **Isaiah 43:1**

BE LIKE CYRUS

There are more than 140 other references in the New Testament to who you are in Christ. God declared these truths about you thousands of years ago!

Be like Cyrus, find yourself in the pages of scripture, and be seized by a holy desire to do God's will and be who God says you are.

Don't waste another minute of your life allowing your status, personality, nationality, religion, possessions, habits, or other's opinions of you to define you. Don't let it consume or affect you if it's not written in the Bible. Always seek identity in your heavenly Father.

You are an original. You are one of a kind. Nobody has your fingerprint, voiceprint, style, flare, grace, or creativity.

The "I AM" statements above come from God's Word, from His knowledge of how you were designed. We often get stuck in a negative mindset, living our lives in the light of the knowledge we gained growing up.

But today, you can decide which one of those identities will prevail on the battlefield of your mind. Will it be what you grew up around? Or will it be what you were created to be? Because the victor of that battle will determine the trajectory of your future.

Have you allowed people to put you in a cubicle of their understanding of you? And has that action exiled you to live the rest of your life according to the names they have assigned to you?

Those false identities will keep you from walking in purpose. Why don't you pray right now and hand those false identity statements to your Heavenly Father? Ask the Heavenly Father what he calls you. What identity or surname has he given you?

When he speaks, it won't be with accusation or in condemnation. He will never address you in a manner that legitimizes a false identity applied to you. The Heavenly Father only calls you by names that He calls Himself. That's how you will know it's him.

He only calls you something that moves you forward into freedom.

CHAPTER 7
CONNECT THE DOTS

Think about this question: What if what happened to you actually happened for you?

Romans 8:28 (NKJV)

> 28And we know that all things work together for
> good to those who love God, to those who are
> the called according to His purpose.

Can I tell you that "things" don't work together? Things will kill you without an overarching purpose, pattern, and plan to it all. The chaos of things will crush you. It takes a word from God to turn chaos into calm and disorder into order.

The New Living Translation catches the true Greek meaning:

> 28And we know that God causes everything to
> work together for the good of those who love

God and are called according to his purpose for them.

The NIV says: *"in all things God works."* You see, things don't work, but God does. He works in everything.

The words "work together" are the Greek words: *sunergei*.

> *Sun* – to with
> *Ernie* – to work

It's where we get our English word Synergize.

The word "good" in this verse is the Greek word *agathos*, which means "good from God's perspective."

God synergizes all things, good things, bad things, big things, little things, ugly things, beautiful things, right things, and wrong things, to work for our good.

With that in mind, let's review the question posed at the outset. What if what happened to you happened for you?

Here is a story that shows you what I am trying to convey with that question.

A person was bitten by an animal and ran to the river to wash out the poison from his wound. While at the river, he saw a child drowning. He jumped into the water and rescued the child. When the child thanked him, he responded, "Don't thank me, thank the animal that bit me. It was his bite that sent me to the river in the first place so that I might be in a position to rescue you."

CONNECT THE DOTS OF YOUR STORY

Here is how you can connect the dots for your own story.

First, you need to believe your story.

Ephesians 2:10 (TPT)

[10]We have become his poetry, a re-created people that will fulfill the destiny he has given each of us, for we are joined to Jesus, the Anointed One. Even before we were born, God planned in advance our destiny and the good works we would do to fulfill it!

From ancient times, storytelling has been a primary medium of communication. The very first words in Genesis confirm that a story is about to be told: "In the beginning God..."

Multiple civilizations have used stories to pass on information, heritage, and truth from generation to generation long before technological multimedia capabilities. Storytelling is the oldest tool of influence in human history. No wonder Jesus, the master teacher, also used this most powerful teaching device.

You can grab the attention of most children by saying quietly, "Once upon a time, there was…"

Each of us has a story, our own individual story. From the beginning, God has been writing each of our stories.

God created each one of us in His image for His glory. He is the one who did the creating. God is all about our story.

You are the only one who can live out the story God intended for you. No one else can have your story. Understanding your individual story as a vehicle for spiritual formation energizes and frees you personally. You are the only one who can bring God glory through your story because it is your unique story.

Can you trust your story?

Your story began before your conception. God was writing your story even before you knew what route the hand of God would take you. God created you for His glory and purposes. You are called to reflect His glory to the world through your story.

Hebrews 11:21 tells us, *"Jacob blessed both the sons of Joseph and worshiped, leaning upon the top of his staff."*

Scholars believe the people of that era would carve their encounters and miracles they had witnessed onto their staff. They would make marks to remember times when the Lord blessed or rescued them. There were moments in his life that were so pivotal and life-changing that he carved a record of those encounters and miracles onto his staff. And then he "leaned on his staff," or you could say, he leaned on his testimonies. He used those markings as a reminder that God had never failed him in the past and that He would be faithful to keep him in his future.

Your story is where your authority comes from. No one can tell you that you didn't experience what you experienced or how it felt to go through what you've been through. No one can convince you that you made it through any other way than by God's grace.

You lean on your testimony, your story. You can point to those crushing and hard times and say, "It was God who brought me through."

The second way to connect the dots is to know that God wastes nothing you've been through.

How have your experiences defined the way you live?

I want to show you three men in the Bible who address the question of how our experiences should define our lives. We will look at Moses, Peter, and Paul.

Moses will represent preparation time for us. Moses' mother made a basket, and his sister, Miriam, placed him at the riverbank (Exodus 2:3). He grew up in Pharaoh's palace and was a prince of Egypt for his first forty years. He spent the next forty years on the backside of the desert. He was a shepherd during those years in the desert, so this meant he knew how to butcher sheep. He was in training and learned how to butcher a lamb, a skill he would later use on the first Passover night. In the wilderness, who would God call to the top of a mountain for forty days to give him the plans of the palace of God? His time in Pharaoh's palace was preparation time for him to understand God's plans for his dwelling place on earth.

Peter represents God's making right our mistakes. He had an incredible journey with Jesus, but he made all kinds of mistakes.

We may recall the occasion wherein he denied Jesus three times after he swore that he wouldn't.

There was the occasion when he chopped off the guy's ear in the garden when a mob came to arrest Jesus. But then, in 2 Peter 1:10, he encourages us to "make all the more certain of your calling." Before these failures, Jesus had called him a rock and prepared Peter to be one of the pillars of the New Testament church.

Peter's mistakes never detoured Jesus from His plan and purpose for Peter's life.

Then there is Paul. Paul represents our encounter with God. Paul had that incredible encounter with Jesus on the Damascus Road. He had been a terrorist in his day, but this commissioning encounter became the benchmark for his ministry.

In **1 Corinthians 2:1**, Paul states: *"I don't come with clever words but the demonstration of power."*

He entered the Christian family through a powerful encounter and demonstrated power throughout the rest of his ministry.

Now, relate these three stories to your stories:

Preparation = Moses

What did you grow up around that prepared you for what God wanted to do in your life? You can look back and see that it was preparing you.

Mistakes = Peter

What mistakes have you made in your life that Jesus wants to make right and use for His glory? God has an extraordinary way of using our failures for our ultimate good. God can use your failings to transform the lives of those around you.

Encounter = Paul

His encounter with Jesus on the Damascus Road (**Acts 9**) changed everything for Paul. Paul's conversion was dramatic and startling. He lived from that encounter. No matter what you encounter, your response should be the same as Paul's. He said, "What do you want me to do?" And thus began his incredible journey. How has your encounter with Jesus, your Redeemer, changed how you live?

The third principle for connecting the dots in our life is this — He redeems the lows.

Job 19:25 says: *"I know that my redeemer lives."*

To redeem something means to return it to its original value. There is no low point in your life that God won't redeem. God is the perfect healer. He didn't send the junk, the pain, or the chaos, but he redeems it.

There's a practice that originated many years ago in Japan called Kintsugi (golden joinery).

It's the art of repairing broken and chipped pottery and ceramics by mending cracks and filling voids using a resin containing gold dust.

When we break things, we might pull out the super glue and try to repair them as seamlessly as possible, hoping they will look like they were never broken.

But Kintsugi does the opposite. It acknowledges the brokenness and articulates and highlights it.

As a philosophy, it treats breakage and repair as part of an object's history rather than something to disguise. The "patch" makes the piece stronger and more valuable.

It acknowledges the history of the brokenness, but through the intricate gold veining that now runs through the pottery, the vessel regains its original purpose—but in a way better and more beautiful than the potter's original idea or intention.

No matter what has happened to you, you have never been past the point of God's ability to renew, regenerate, and repurpose it all. God has been the potter, and you are His clay.

You may have suffered through trauma, pain, and disappointment and felt cracked, broken, and shattered.

Each life experience, each trauma, each crack, and each flaw has served as a lesson for you. They have taught you something. They have taught you to rely more fully on God; they have taught you to have hope even in the darkest darkness.

What our culture calls flaws and imperfections, what our culture teaches us to hide, God covers with gold. God highlights and makes those areas holy.

God says your scars and imperfections are beautiful. God says they are gifts, and He uses your greater vulnerability, strength, and hope to bless the world.

He wastes nothing **(Romans 8:28),** absolutely nothing, and He gets you ready for adventures you never would have dreamed possible.

He redeems the lows!

In John chapter 9, there is a story about a blind man who was blind from birth. The disciples asked the inevitable question, "Master, who sinned so horribly that this man was born blind? Was it he or his parents?"

They believed someone had to be at fault.

Notice the direction of the disciples' inquiry. They look toward the past for the answer to the problem. They focus on the causes of the effect. Something or someone must be responsible, so they needed Jesus to tell them who or what caused this to happen.

But Jesus looks in an entirely different direction. He pays absolutely no attention to finding the meaning of this event in the past. He replies that no one is to blame. What? Does this mean there wasn't any cause for this blindness? Of course not!

There was a cause, but Jesus says the explanation is not found by looking for a cause. It is to be found by looking for a purpose!

It's not what happened that matters. What matters is what is going to happen!

This man's ailment served as a vehicle for revealing God's glory!

In most of our human experiences, we look into the past to find an answer to the present question, "WHY?" Why did this happen to me? And as we stand, like the disciples, sorting through the past to find the causal chain of events needed to explain the meaning of some present set of circumstances, Jesus calls a halt to the whole methodology! The meaning of it cannot be explained from an examination of a past casual chain of events. The meaning must come from a future purpose!

My present circumstances cannot be understood according to the actions that brought them into being. They can only be understood according to their ultimate fulfillment of God's eternal purposes. And that purpose includes revealing the glory of God.

It wasn't that he or his parents had sinned; he was a miracle waiting to happen. He's been blind all his life but will be healed so that God might receive glory. He didn't sin. It's that the works of God should be revealed in him.

What had happened to him in the past, his blindness, actually happened for him to glorify God in the present!

Can God use any suffering you've experienced to bring out a greater good in your life? Yes!!! He wastes nothing!

EMBRACING YOUR STORY

You need to see yourself in the middle of your story and truly set apart to bring God glory. You may prefer something else to your story. No one would have voluntarily chosen pain, difficulty, or the particular parts that have been hurtful and damaging. But because of redemption, we have the choice to embrace our story, as difficult as it may be, or to resist it. God uses our stories, the good and the bad, to bring Him the utmost glory.

What parts of your story have you yet to embrace? How does the Lord want you to respond to the insight He has given you through the processing of your life story? What is He calling you to be and to do?

Believe your story. He redeems the lows. He wastes nothing. He gets you ready for glorious things!

In **John 9:25**, the Pharisees kept asking this man if Jesus was a sinner. He states in verse 25, *"I don't know if he's a sinner or not, but one thing I do know, that though I was blind, now I see!"*

Leonard Ravenhill once said, "A man with an experience of God is never at the mercy of a man with an argument."

And the last principle for connecting the dots of your life is this: He repeats the highs.

Revelation 19:10b (TPT) *"The testimony of Jesus is the spirit of prophecy."*

Our testimony carries with it God's desire to do it again. The testimony of Jesus is the spirit of prophecy.

Your victories are your story, and your story becomes your testimony. Our stories of our victories can give others experiences to emulate.

According to Webster's Dictionary, the verb emulate means to match or surpass (a person or achievement), typically by imitation.

Your story provides a basis for others to relate to you and to root for you.

Fanny Crosby wrote the hymn "Blessed Assurance," which contains the phrase: "This is my story; this is my song. Praising my Savior, all the day long."

Despite being blind, she wrote more than 8,000 hymns. And those hymns have been copied more than 100 million times.

She had a story about her Savior, and it released her song. She said on her deathbed that had she not been blind, she may have been too distracted by the things around her to write such songs.

We may never write a song that will be sung like Fanny Crosby's is, but we are not writing for that reason.

Take notice of the places in your life where the enemy fights you the hardest. Where you face the most warfare usually indicates where the enemy is the most afraid. The place where he attacks you reveals where he feels most vulnerable to you.

2 Corinthians 2:14 (TPT)

[14]God always makes his grace visible in Christ,
who includes us as partners of his endless

triumph. Through our yielded lives he spreads
the fragrance of the knowledge of God
everywhere we go.

Later in the story of the blind man in John 9, it states that he had been blind for 40 years. What if your 40-year-old problem is a setup for someone else's miracle, breakthrough, or salvation?

Remember, your story is a way for God to let others know that He wants to "do it again" for them as well.

> Believe your story.
> God wastes nothing.
> He redeems your lows.
> He repeats your highs.

What if what happened to you happened so that the glory of God could be revealed?

WORKS CITED

"G3875 - Paraklētos - Strong's Greek Lexicon (NIV)." Blue
　　Letter Bible,
　　www.blueletterbible.org/lexicon/g3875/niv/mgnt/0-1/.

Hackett, Conrad. *Christians Remain World's Largest Religious
　　Group, but They Are Declining in Europe,* Pew Research
　　Center, 5 Apr. 2017, www.pewresearch.org/short-
　　reads/2017/04/05/christians-remain-worlds-largest-
　　religious-group-but-they-are-declining-in-
　　europe/#:~:text=Christians%20remained%20the%20la
　　rgest%20religious%20group%20in%20the,to%20a%2
　　0new%20Pew%20Research%20Center%20demographi
　　c%20analysis.

Hegg, Tim. "Hebrew Word Yada." *TorahResource,* 8 May 2024,
　　torahresource.com/article/hebrew-word-yada/.

McCollam, Dan. *Basic Training for Prophetic Activation.* iWAR
　　and Sounds of the Nation, 2012.

*More Than 300,000 Estimated Victims of Human Trafficking in
　　Texas,* The University of Texas at Austin - Steve Hicks
　　School of Social Work, 11 Oct. 2020,

socialwork.utexas.edu/more-than-300000-estimated-victims-of-human-trafficking-in-texas/.

Sex Trafficking in the U.S.: A Closer Look at U.S. Citizen ..., Polaris, polarisproject.org/wp-content/uploads/2019/09/us-citizen-sex-trafficking.pdf.

RESOURCES FOR FURTHER STUDY

The Mirror Study Bible

Dr. Ron Cottle Resources – www.roncottle.com

In Pursuit of Purpose **by Dr. Myles Monroe**

Find Your Why **by Simon Sinek**

Living Fearless **by Jamie Winship**

PaulManwaring.com

Hebrew Word Study: Skip Moen - www.skipmoen.com

Chaim Bentorah - www.chaimbentorah.com

Why You Want to Study the Bible, and Transcend Religion - www.abarim-publications.com

ABOUT THE AUTHOR

Dr. Susan Nordin serves as campus pastor at the Houston location of Community Transformation Church. She serves alongside her husband, Pastor Don Nordin, who serves as the lead pastor.

CT Church is a multicultural and multigenerational congregation that has grown to encompass nine campuses under their leadership.

Susan holds a Bachelor of Ministry from the Central Christian University of North Carolina. She recently earned her Master of Ministry and Doctor of Sacred Studies with Embassy College based in Columbus, Georgia. She draws inspiration, wisdom, and compassion from her 40-plus years of experience in the ministry.

Susan is the author of *One Determined Mom*, a 30-day devotional for modern moms. She also participated in *The Invitation*, a devotional book for fifty-one other ladies from around the country.

She serves as the vice president of Global Ministries Network (gmnonline.org), which credentials ministers and oversees the work of member churches.

Susan also serves as the president of Project Hope Recovery Center and Saving Grace Recovery Center, year-long residential rehabilitation ministries for men and women with life-controlling problems. Project Hope and Saving Grace have eight centers in five states and can house up to 220 students at any time.

Most recently, Pastor Susan became the President & CEO of The Haven, which is a ministry that rescues minors (8-17 years old) who have been sex trafficked.

Susan travels extensively conducting women's conferences, revivals, marriage seminars, board and staff training, teaches effective church structures, and much more!

Susan and her husband host the Empowerment Conference at Community Transformation Church each year. The conference is a top-tier preaching and resourcing event that draws hundreds of ministers worldwide and features some of the premier speakers in today's Pentecostal circles.

Susan loves personal time with Scripture, reading, decorating, and shopping.

For more information about Dr. Susan Nordin or how to craft your purpose statement, please visit thenordins.org.

Made in the USA
Middletown, DE
04 September 2024

59745561R00066